For Uncle Cal and Auntie Anne
—T.H.

For Goldie
—W.H.

Waldman House Press
525 North Third Street
Minneapolis, Minnesota 55401

Up to the Lake

by Tom Hegg
illustrated by Warren Hanson

Waldman House Press

INTRODUCTION

Minnesota Seasons are quite given to extremes...
From Winter's arctic wind-chills to the Summer's tropic steams...
From the gushing blooms of Springtime to the blazing hues of Fall...
It's murder on our siding...then again, we have it all.

Living in this latitude at times is rather rough,
But with the proper attitude, it isn't all that tough...
And prodigals who've trod the globe in search of greener lands
Return each day with eyes downcast and threadbare hats in hands.

I'd like to share some stories that have always brought me joy;
Of Summers in the Northwoods when I was a growing boy...
Of crystal lakes and pines and sunnies tugging on a hook...
And characters to love forever...if you buy the book.

T.H.

GETTING THERE

Next year, we're going to get it right...
We'll plan so we can travel light.

There's no good reason, is there dear,
To load the car with tons of gear...

Of course we need the things we use,
But really...twenty pairs of shoes?

And must the kids bring every toy?
I didn't when I was a boy—

...I don't care what my mother said;
You might believe the man you wed!

...Go ahead and laugh...that's fine...
But next year, better half of mine,

Next year we're going to get it right...
We'll plan so we can travel light.

GETTING CLOSE…

We'll be there in a little while…
Let's hold our breath for one whole mile!
…I know we did that game before…
Now, settle down! Not one word more.

…Yes, I know they're tired and bored…
I win the Grumpy Dad award…
I'm sorry, kids. Your dad's a schmoo.
I'm not? Okay. I love you, too.

Say! What's the first thing on your list?
Fishing? Swimming?…I got kissed!
Who dat kiss me on the cheek?
Who dat kiss 'dis ol' antique?

Hey, look! Our turn off, dead ahead!
Let's all unpack and go to bed!
…Only kidding!…half-past noon…
Yes, we'll be there very soon.…

Would someone move that cooler, please!
That squeaking drives me crazy! Geeze!
Thanks. I…what? I did not swear!
I only said…well, split a hair!

Come on, hon…please, let's not fight…
I just…Oh, great! The engine light!
I had it serviced back in town…
I laid two hundred dollars down!

Yes, of course the tank is filled...
It isn't gas, it's...Swell! It killed!
That smell...we've had a hose explode...
We've got to get it off the road.

Here, take the wheel. I'll go push...
Kids, stay put! I'll smack your tush!
It's dangerous! Stay where you are!
Dad can move the doggone car...

...What?...In neutral, not in gear!
...We might get there some time this year...
...Ungh!...It's moving...turn the wheel!
(The guy says, "This car is a steal!"

The blasted thing's a steal, allright...
I was robbed, in broad daylight.)
...Whew!...All clear...okay, climb out...
STAY OFF THE ROAD!...I DID NOT SHOUT!

Yes, this air is fresh and sweet...
Do we have anything to eat?
Ham sandwiches...that's perfect, love...
Mm! Good as manna from above...

Wait a sec...here comes a truck...
HOWDY...YEAH, WE'RE OUT OF LUCK...
...YOU CAN? OH, THANKS! BOY, THAT'S JUST GREAT!
...He's got a rig to haul this crate!

OUR PLACE IS JUST A LITTLE WAY...
MY FRIEND, YOU REALLY SAVED THE DAY...
KIDS, YOU GET UP IN THE BACK...
SAY, SHOULD THAT CHAIN BE TAUT OR SLACK?

HEY, YOU GOT IT!...That was quick.
You used to this? That's mighty slick.
You live here long? Oh, all your life...
Please, may I introduce my wife...

No, just a couple weeks is all...
The kids start school in early fall.
You take the next right past the sign...
...Oh, you don't have to...this is fine...

My word...that's awfully good of you.
...Yes, it is. We love the view.
...Oh, thanks. My Father built the place.
He really knew from nails and space.

My Brother keeps it in repair...
I couldn't build a house of air.
...This is perfect. Thanks a lot.
...Please, let me see just what I've got...

...We've got to pay you. I insist.
It's just a token...don't resist...
But...I hardly know what I should say...
This doesn't happen every day!

My friend, I think you're quite a guy.
THANKS AGAIN...YOU BET...GOODBYE!...
Hello, cabin. Well...we're back.
Come on, Family. Let's unpack.

PERFECT MOMENT #1: MORNING

I glance at the clock...take a deep, filling yawn...
I make out the dock in the first light of dawn...

The sap-sweetened air is delicious and cool...
The snap of the maple branch burning for fuel...

The lake starts to sparkle with rays from the sun...
The songbirds are singing...and day has begun.

Ma Duck and her brood on a Morning Explore...
The wash of the waves on the rocks of the shore...

My cane-pole alive with the tug of a fish...
The hug of my down-vest...what more could I wish?

THE DOG

Get off the bed, you crazy dog!
Be quiet—go lie down—
It's way too early to get up...
You don't do this in town.

Allright, allright, I'm coming...whoa!
Is this floor ever cold!
Hey—may I get my shoes on, please?
Now, sit! Do as you're told!

Good morning...no, go back to sleep.
The beastie just wants out...
He does this every year...can't wait
To run and sniff and scout.

Morning, kids...yes, Daddy knows
It isn't very light.
...Okay, but do it quietly...
...And promise not to fight!

Honey, don't get up...
...They're going fishing off the dock.
We can wait for breakfast—
Get a load of that old clock.

You relax. I'll walk the dog...
I ought to stretch my legs.
And, if the truth were known, I'd kill
For bacon and fried eggs.

Oh, bless you, honey. You're the best
Of all the Northwoods cooks...
Now, tell me why you married ME...
My money or my looks?

...Allright, allright, I'm going...
Come on, boy...let's get some air.
She's at the stove already—
We have little time to spare.

The breeze is downright bracing...
Good...it's coming from the west...
The clouds have started clearing...
Bit of luck—that's much the best.

Hey, boy...you want to tug-o'-war?
Look here! I've got a stick!
Ugh! You're pretty strong you are...
Leggo—let's do your trick.

Give it...give it...that's a boy,
Okay, you take your stretch...
Now stay...stay...watch it—there it goes!
Go get it, boy—go fetch!

Gosh! He's fast! Unless I knew,
I'd swear he was a pup...
There it is—what's wrong with you?
It's right there...pick it up!

Now what's he doing? Here, boy!...
No! No! No! Come out of there!
What's he got? A bone? A fish?
A porcupine? A bear?

Here, boy!…There he is!…Here, boy!
Say, what got into you?
You daft old thing, you scared me…
Why on earth did…Oh, Pee-ooo!

Get down! Get down! Get off of me!
You rolled in something dead!
You foul cur—for this I left
A warm, sweet-smelling bed…

Let's get back…forget that
Silly stick, for goodness sake…
Kids! Please call the dog…Don't touch him!
…Get him in the lake!

There…Hello, again. Guess what the stupid…
Oh, you heard.
…The smells up here do vary,
From sublime down to absurd.

Right now, the frying bacon
And the coffee smell just fine…
The scents of breakfast mingle with
The tingle of the pine…

…Let me help…I hate to be a
Mere bump on a log.
Tomorrow, I'll do breakfast chores…
(If you will walk the dog).

GRANDPA'S HANDS

Grandpa's hands were big and tanned...
Far darker than the wedding band that hooped
His finger; (twice as grand as any tootsie roll).

How did digits of such size
Together with his "failing eyes" create
The tiny fishing flies he tied? What great control...

Grandpa whittled when he could...
His hands and knife gave life to wood, and birds
Emerged from blocks and stood upon the verge of flight.

Grandpa's hands could mend and fix...
Or bend and snap the strongest sticks. His hands
Could tickle us with tricks before our prayers at night.

Grandpa's hands had built a store,
And Grandpa's hands had gone to war. His hands
Were working long before they ever should have been.

Our cabin is his hand-made dream...
Each brick and block and board and beam. It's so
Much more than it may seem; you've got to look again.

Grandpa's hands are everywhere...
They fashioned every turn and stair. They gave
A shape to Summer's air. They gave us all so much...

Grandpa's hands may be at rest,
But we will be forever blessed, for hands
That did their loving best can never lose their touch.

PERFECT MOMENT #2: MIDDAY

A fresh breeze blows off of the lake and receives
The laughter and happy applause of the leaves...

And now, new-born waves are surprising the sand;
Rising and breaking...baptising the land.

The clouds in the blowing blue plume full and rise
In cumulus majesty...riding the skies.

Now, hear the most wild and primeval of runes...
The coloratura "halloos" of the loons.

It's earth, water, bird and sky caught in a kiss.
I wonder if Heaven will be quite like this...

BIG RED

Big Red's Bait and Tackle Shop is out on Route Eighteen...
Red herself holds forth each day like some great, earthy queen.

Her name comes from the flaming hair atop her hennaed head;
Lacquered into BOO-fahnts, it is quite profoundly—Red.

Her laughter is infectious...it begins with a high wheeze
And builds into a liquid hack that echoes through the trees.

She dresses in bright colors and her make-up is intense;
She seems a bird of paradise perched on a picket fence.

Her figure is, well...generous. Could "healthy" be the word?
Her taste in costume jewelry is nigh unto absurd.

And though she is "exotic" in an outward sort of way,
She has a heart of gold...and I do not mean gold lamé.

My folks first drove in years ago to get some odds and ends,
And after one trip to Big Red's, we were her life-long friends.

She had to know our names. She had to know how old we were...
And where we planned to stay—and for how long—was Big to her.

She gave out fishing tips and told a bawdy joke or two,
And had us all in love with her before she was quite through.

She netted minnows from her purring tanks with deftest ease;
Broke popsicles in half—by hand—as if that feat's a breeze.

And though her place was well away from fast-delivery routes,
She got the latest comics—(she said we were "in cahoots").

She has a bit of everything inside her little store...
Mousetraps...chainsaws...bacon...miscellaneous and more.

She is a Justice of the Peace...a Notary, as well...
And just how old SHE is, we'll never know—she'll never tell.

She's still there, with her sculptured BOO-fahnt
    riding on her head...
And now MY kids are quick to say, "Dad—let's go see Big Red!"

SQUALL

The thunderheads of greenish-black are forming in the west,
And aspens raise their leaves in quick surrender to the test.

The ripples on the lake are being whipped up into waves…
The waves bend into whitecaps like so many bowing slaves.

We race to take the snapping laundry off the dancing line
While eyeing, apprehensively, that giant pitching pine…

The first fat drops hit heavily and darken spots of dirt…
They coldly fix my gooseflesh to my once-loose cotton shirt.

The vivid, frightening lightning bolts first flash—and then explode!
We make the cabin just in time…here comes the Mother Lode.

The drumming on the roof becomes a thrumming, numbing roar…
The wall of falling water washes off the forest floor.

I tell the kids that all is well despite the churning skies…
They say, "Then how come we can see the whites all 'round your eyes?"

And then, almost as quickly as the tempest had begun,
The rain lets up…and clouds are split by beams of yellow sun.

A sense of calm and sweet relief comes sweeping through the room…
It's safe to say we love it when the sky stops going boom.

And now, with boats to bail out and branches we must clear,
We go to work with grateful smiles that stretch from ear to ear.

Sometimes we need a sudden squall to thunder through the pine…
I wonder why it helps to put priorities in line?

NOTHING'S PERFECT

Well, sure...there are a few things I don't love about the place...
Like unseen spider filaments that drape across your face.

And oversize mosquitos—ever numerous and near—
That hum sustained high C's at night while dancing 'round your ear.

And yes, I must confess that I am none too fond of bats.
They have this way of folding up and slipping through the slats...

And leeches! Just the sight of one can make me go all green.
The very thought of what they do is perfectly obscene.

But even with this host of things that crawl and flit and ooze,
There isn't a vacation spot on Earth I'd rather choose.

SONG OF THE SCREEN DOOR

The screen door sings a homey song
Of cozy creaks and crangs

That kids just love to punctuate
With nerve-exploding bangs...

They wait until you're nodding off...
(As grown-ups often do)

Or better, 'til your coffee cup
Is full of scalding brew.

And then, just as if shot from guns
At deadly point-blank range...

Wham! They're in!...Or, slam! They're out!
And splash!...You have to change.

BIG BEE

I'm certain I will never see
A bigger, fatter honeybee...

His girth is nothing less than great
And daisies give beneath his weight!

Now, normally, I'd run inside.
But somehow, I don't want to hide...

In fact, I'm duty-bound to stay...
(Such bees you don't see every day).

I can't believe a bee that size
Can even move...but this one flies!

That really is the oddest thing...
He's like a hippo on the wing.

It seems as if his yellow vest
Might be too tight across his chest...

...My word...there's black fur on his face.
His buzzing sounds like russian bass...

We sure do grow 'em big up here.
Is something in the atmosphere?

He's taking off...don't sting me, please!
Now...do I run, or do I freeze?

Oh, look...I guess he's got the goods...
He's humming home, deep in the woods.

He's gone. Well, I feel quite relieved.
That bee was not to be believed!

I doubt that I'd say this aloud,
But in a way, I'm rather proud...

To think that our own humble trees
Are home to world-class bumble-bees.

JOAN AND MARV

"MARRRRV!"
The call came shrilling through the forest's gentle hum...
"DON'T FORGET THEM OSPREYS! TIE A STRING AROUND YOUR THUMB!"

The voice was unmistakable; the edge could make you cringe...
A cross between a siren, Ethel Merman and a hinge.

She sees me. "IS THAT TOMMY HEGG? GOOD LORD, BOY! YOU HAVE GROWN!"
Her volume full when nose to nose. That's how it was with Joan.

"Good morning, Mrs. Miller. May I buy a couple things?"
SURE! SURE! COME IN!" She pivots 'round...
    the pounding sound just rings.

"MARV WENT TO RESCUE OSPREY BABIES! SOMEONE SHOT THEIR MA!
SAY DID YOU HEAR ABOUT THE TIME..." She's off again... Tra-la!

On top of vocal power, she could ramble on at length
With no apparent end to her invention's artless strength.

You could stand, quite poised to leave, with one foot out the door
And Joan could hold you captive as she loudly held the floor.

Your only hope—perhaps another soul might wander in;
Could be the well-worn phone will buzz and catch her merry din.

Or better, maybe Marv himself will come back from his rounds...
(Joan reserved for him alone the choicest of her sounds.)

Joan and Marvin Miller; wife and husband since The Flood...
They built a tidy business with their muscles, sweat and blood.

A string of ten log cabins and the massive old Main Lodge...
Some rowboats and a tackle house and Marv's black truck...a Dodge.

These, plus Joan's Convenience Store made up their fine resort,
And work, they did...
    while patrons lounged or gave themselves to sport.

I scarcely did see Marv without some load upon his back,
Or sweating over something that had "Done gone outta whack."

Marv was not a big man. Nor a young man. He was proud...
And every bit as quiet as his loving wife was loud.

And though they worked around the clock (not just from sun to sun),
One sensed that as they labored, they were having lots of fun...

Marv took us on fishing trips to hidden Vesper Lake...
(Yes, we were touristas and yes, Marv was on the make.)

But even if cold profit was the motivating force,
His pleasure at OUR pleasure welled up from a warmer source.

Joan would love to come along, if business would allow,
And she'd be in her glory holding court up in the bow.

Their old resort has passed now to some younger, stronger hands...
I'll think of it as Joan and Marv's as long as it still stands...

And when I hear a piercing voice resound around the lake,
I'll hear the mighty tones of Joan...
    and cringe, for old time's sake.

BEAN-HOLE BEANS

Salt pork...onions...stone-white beans...
    molasses, to be sure.
Dry mustard and brown sugar
    for a dark, sweet, nutty cure.
All tightly covered in a two-quart
    cast-iron cooking pot,
And buried four feet deep in hardwood coals,
    all glowing-hot.

Bean-hole beans are being born...
    you dare not rush them, though...
Half the day must pass while they are
    bubbling below.
Giddy expectation must sustain us
    'til they're done.
But in the Northwoods, getting there
    is truly half the fun.

For elders tell the children
    of the dish's history...
Of voyageurs and trappers...
    wonder, warmth and mystery.
Soon, everyone is purposefully
    bustling about...
And then, it's dusk...it's time for us
    to go and dig them out.

At last, they're here...we brush the ashes,
     slowly lift the lid...
The drama of it all grabs every grown-up
     and each kid...
And, oh! The rich aroma in that piping
     puff of steam...
In rapid, glad response, assembled mouths
     begin to stream.

The beans are jewel-perfect;
     each a warm, translucent brown.
And self-control is lost
     as all your taste buds go to town.
Bean-hole beans...the best things
     ever buried under coals...
The flavors introduced, betrothed
     and married deep in holes.

"Without advanced devices,
     sans all classes in cuisine,
In the presence of these spices,
     I, Molasses, take thee, Bean."
Mmm's and aah's are everywhere,
     and praise is heaped upon...
Beans being what they are,
     we'll hear yet more of them anon.

PERFECT MOMENT #3: EVENING

The tree-tops catch the last few rays of sunset's red-gold light…
The Lake's a liquid mirror, giving back the glowing sight.

A big-dog bark is echoing…an outboard motor bawls…
A loon elates the evening air with thrilling, mystic calls…

Supper sizzles busily and kindles appetites…
The kids are playing—quietly—and steering clear of fights.

A rap upon the screen door…our best friends have come to call!
The rarest, dearest people…welcome anytime at all…

A sense of purest pleasure fills the cabin through and through…
A bit of life to treasure…moments perfect, moments few.

SUMMER CRUSH

She sent me into transports of the most
        exquisite agony and joy...
How could feelings this intense be housed
        within the confines of one boy?

I met her...well, I saw her at Big Red's...
        she looked so radiantly bored...
Everything about her was perfection...
        I was stunned...no, I was floored.

She flipped through magazines with vague disinterest
        as her folks gassed up their car...
Her father looked athletic
        and her mother could have been a movie star...

But she was clearly greater than the sum
        of those two formidable parts...
And then, she glanced at me...it hit...
        like poison from some pygmy's potent darts.

The meeting of our eyes was fleeting; still,
*   it rocked me with volcanic force...*
I shuddered with sweet nausea...
*   my pulse was pounding like a charging horse.*

My knees had gone to jelly
*   and my head was ringing like a tuning-fork...*
Like overcharged champagne,
*   I felt as if I was about to pop my cork...*

And then, she looked away...
*   she frowned a bit, as if offended by the sight...*
Our romance was a mere look old, but lo...
*   the awful truth had come to light...*

The feeling wasn't mutual.
*   But then again, how could it ever be?*
She was...all the things she was,
*   and I was stuck with being only me.*

I cursed my imperfections and rehearsed them
     in self-pitying detail...
I tossed upon a sea of adolescent drama,
     trauma and travail...

And just as I'd begun to quite enjoy my black
     and bottomless despair,
My Mother's voice came drilling
     through the killing hot and humid August air.

"TOM-MEEEEE!" She insisted,
     in the tones one used to call a child of five.
I knew if I resisted,
     seconds later she, herself, would then arrive.

In hot humiliation, I obeyed the voice
     and made to leave the store...
And stopped dead in my paces at the sight I saw
     beyond Big Red's screen door.

Mom and Mrs. Movie Star were chatting
    like the very best of friends!
Dad and Mr. Athlete were laughing!
    I felt like I had the bends...

And to my horror, Dad then called me over
    to the chuckling quartet...
I can't recall all names,
    but the events...I'm sure I never will forget.

"Tommy, this is So-and-so,
    and this is Mrs. So-and-so, his wife."
"Very pleased to meet you."
    (Biggest lie I ever told in my whole life!)

"Say, you must meet Cyndi Ann!
    She's just about your age now, I should think!"
The strong man called his daughter...
    I began to flush an iridescent pink.

Cyndi Ann came over at a brisk, good-natured,
    unself-conscious trot...
She met my Folks quite graciously...
    and then, their son...whom heaven had forgot.

She said, "Hi." in a cool, controlled contralto
    that could make Kahlua freeze...
My voice cracked like Alfalfa's did
    when reaching for the high notes in "Louise".

I then attained a state of deep embarrassment
    so painful and so pure,
A stay with Eastern Monks in far-off mountains was, I felt,
    the only cure.

But after an eternity of talking with the So-and-so's,
    they left...
Leaving me relieved,
    but at the same time, feeling empty and bereft.

I'd love that girl forever.
    This was not, as Dad suggested, "just a phase".
I'd love that girl eternally...
    at least, for a good couple-three more days...

PERFECT MOMENT #4: NIGHTTIME

Reading at night in a single light...
Everyone else is asleep.
Private delight in a pool of white...
Pillows all downy and deep.

Cozy in bed with a book half read...
Got it propped up on my knees.
Eyelids of lead in a nodding head...
Cool of a rain-scented breeze.

Been on this page for what seems an age...
Read the same sentence ten times.
I'm at that stage where I can't quite gauge
Repentence apart from the crimes...

Can't even think...just a blur of ink
Is winking at me through the haze...
I'm on the brink...one more yawn or blink
And...(this book may take a few days.)

BACK TO TOWN

Next year, we're going to get it right...
We'll plan, so we can travel light.

...Go ahead and laugh...that's fine...
But next year, better half of mine...

Next year, we're going to get it right...
We'll plan, so we can travel light.